CIRCE & BRAVO

Also by Donald Freed

Plays
Inquest
Faust in Harlem
Secret Honor (with Arnold M. Stone)
The White Crow
The Countess
Villa!
Solidarity!
Alfred and Victoria (A Life)
The Quartered Man
Shakespeare (with Geoff Forward)
The Gandhi Problem (with Harold Lieberman)
The Horatio Alger Show (with Harold Lieberman)
The Last Hero

Books
Freud and Stanislavski
The Existentialism of Alberto Moravia (with Joan Ross)
Agony in New Haven
The Spymaster
The China Card
Death in Washington
The Killing of RFK
Executive Action (with Mark Lane)
The Secret Life of Ronald Reagan
The Glasshouse Tapes (Editor)
Big Brother and the Holding Company (Editor)
In Search of Common Ground (with Huey P. Newton and Erik H. Erikson)

Screenplays
Executive Action (with Mark Lane and Dalton Trumbo)
Television on Trial
Secret Honor

DONALD FREED

CIRCE & BRAVO

AMBER LANE PRESS

All rights whatsoever in this play are strictly reserved and application for performance, etc. must be made before rehearsals begin to:
Rochelle Stevens & Co.
114 Upper Street
Islington
London N1 1QN

No performance may be given unless a licence has been obtained.

First published in 1986 by
Amber Lane Press Ltd.
9 Middle Way
Oxford OX2 7LH

Typeset in Ehrhardt by
Oxford Computer Typesetting

Printed and manufactured in Great Britain by
Cotswold Press Ltd., Oxford

Copyright © Donald Freed, 1986

ISBN: 0 906399 74 2

CONDITIONS OF SALE
This book is sold subject to the condition that it shall not, by way of trade or otherwise, be lent, re-sold, hired out or otherwise circulated without the publisher's prior consent in any form of binding or cover other than that in which it is published and without a similar condition including this condition being imposed on the subsequent purchaser.

Circe & Bravo is dedicated to Patty

"...and let me speak to the yet unknowing world
How these things came about. So shall you hear
Of carnal, bloody and unnatural acts,
Of accidental judgement, casual slaughters —
And, in this upshot, purposes mistook
Fall'n on the inventor."

Hamlet

"WASHINGTON: On the orders of the Reagan Administration, the Pentagon last week completed a strategic master plan to give the United States the capability of winning a protracted nuclear war with the Soviet Union, The Times has learned."

The Los Angeles Times

"About $230 million is being spent to renovate the Statue of Liberty in New York harbor, but when the famous symbol of freedom has its coming out party July 4, one sign of aging will still be there.

Miss Liberty, who has greeted millions of immigrants of all races and nationalities, is turning black.

'There is nothing that can be done about it,' said Robert Baboian, a corrosion expert and consultant to the U.S. Park Service on the restoration of the statue."

The Los Angeles Times

Circe & Bravo was first given an experimental or "Equity Waiver" production in April 1984 at the Met Theatre in Los Angeles, California. It was produced and directed by Paul Koslo with the following cast:

    CIRCE: .... Barbara Rae
    BRAVO: .... James Broome

The first regional theatre production of *Circe & Bravo* was in April 1985 at the Denver Theatre Center. It was produced by Donovan Marley and directed by Laird Williamson with the following cast:

    CIRCE: .... Leslie Lyles
    BRAVO: .... Byron Jennings

Circe & Bravo was first produced in England at the Hampstead Theatre, London, on 5 June 1986. It was directed by Harold Pinter with the following cast:

    CIRCE: .... Faye Dunaway
    BRAVO: .... Stephen Jenn

    Set Designer: Eileen Diss
    Costumes: Jane Robinson
    Lighting: Mick Hughes
    Music/Sound: Dominic Muldowney

CHARACTERS

CIRCE   The First Lady.

BRAVO   A Secret Service Agent.

TIME: The 1980s.

PLACE: The President of the United States' and the First Lady's lodge at Camp David Mountain Retreat.

ACT ONE: Late afternoon.

ACT TWO: Night.

ACT ONE

Setting: A Government Issue natural wood lodge, Camp David, Maryland. Entrance U.R., bedroom U.C., kitchenette area on L. There are chairs, a coffee table, a desk. Some of the furniture is circa 1940 to 1955. There is also a JFK-style rocking chair. A couch, C., faces out. The large windows are covered by heavy, expensive drapes. There is a low fire burning in the fireplace, D.R. The walls are flecked with official citations and pictures. It is a cold, "modern," official lodge. There is an old-fashioned wall clock. Stuffed game hangs about the walls, and there are various American-Indian carvings and other souvenirs.

In the dark silence before the curtain rises we hear Copland's "Fanfare for the Common Man." Dimly, then, we hear a helicopter approaching. This chopping sound is the audio emblem of the play.

The cold winter light comes up to 4 p.m. as the chopper roars in and out.

Music holds.

A SECRET SERVICE AGENT (BRAVO), *with a wire in his ear, enters and moves quickly to check out the lodge. He is young, fair, lithe, moves like a killer. He is bare-headed and wears reflecting dark glasses, black leather gloves, and a trench-coat open down the front.*

He opens the drapes wider to catch the day's last light. Then he disappears into the bedroom, returns, checks out the kitchenette, and crosses to C. *He jots an entry into a small black book.*

He stands rigid before turning and kneeling by the fireplace. He takes a poker, heats the tip in the flames, and twirls it like a cheerleader. Then, he removes one black glove and makes as if to press the palm of his hand against the red hot tip of the poker.

Suddenly the walkie-talkie sputters static.

WALKIE-TALKIE VOICE: This is "Able-Tower", Able-Tower. Come in. Bravo. Bravo, come in! Do you copy?

> [*The helicopter moves back into hearing range.* BRAVO *leaps to his feet, puts on his glove, and becomes robotized again. He speaks into an invisible electronic module in his jacket.*]

BRAVO: This is "B" for "Bravo". "Bravo" to "Able". Bravo to Able. Bravo to Able. Come in, Able. Do you copy?

WALKIE-TALKIE VOICE: This is Able. "Circe" is in the compound. Circe is in the compound. Do you copy, Bravo?

BRAVO: I copy. Quarters secure. Over.

WALKIE-TALKIE VOICE: Circe is in the compound. Proceed until 1700 hours.

> [BRAVO *exits to the road outside, where a vehicle can be heard arriving. Car doors slam. The First Lady, the President of the United States' wife — code-name "Circe" — enters.* CIRCE *is near fifty but looks a good ten years younger. She is a former beauty queen who has earned, decades after having been selected as "Miss LSU," an electric ambience of sensuality and suffering and an unforgettable style of doomed glamor. Her eyes and voice could be those of a great tragic actress, and her sensibility that of a doomed, damned poet or a grand and flaming courtesan.*

She projects elegance, and superb taste: textured wool, soft silk, supple leather and is, idiosyncratically, striking, down to her crafted boots. Alone, CIRCE *strides to the desk, picks up the white telephone receiver and waits for a connection. Outside the helicopter roars. Behind her,* BRAVO *enters with suitcases. He touches her elbow.*]

BRAVO: May I take your coat, Ma'am?

[CIRCE *spins in terror, staring into* BRAVO's *black glasses; she recovers and shouts over the sound of the retreating helicopter. At first, because of the noise, we can only see their lips moving. Finally* —]

CIRCE: ...No thank you, Darlin'. The wind-chill factor is, ah, greater here than at the White House, ah, if you can conceive of that. Hah!

BRAVO: Beg your pardon, Ma'am, I...

[CIRCE *puts down the receiver.*]

CIRCE: I say, no thank you, hon. I don't intend to stay...I'm trying to contact the President, to, ah — "raise the Chief," A — ha...

BRAVO: Shall I put your bags in the —?

CIRCE: Anywhere, and bring me a drink... It's Mr Jerrems, isn't it? All you gentlemen from the Secret Service —

BRAVO: Negative.

[*The helicopter retreats.*]

CIRCE: No? Didn't you intercede between my husband and what the press called a "deceased cat" at Disneyworld? I remember you moved like the wind, balletic...

[*As* BRAVO *carries the baggage to the bedroom his walkie-talkie suddenly squawks.*]

WALKIE-TALKIE VOICE: Able to Bravo, Able to Bravo: Confirm Circe secure, confirm Circe secure. Do you copy?
BRAVO: [*from the bedroom*] I copy, Able. Secure. Secure. Bravo over and out.
[*With the stealth of a big cat* CIRCE *picks up the white telephone again and listens.* BRAVO *re-enters the main room.* CIRCE *is staring at him, the telephone receiver replaced in its cradle. She flicks the rocking chair; it creaks as it rocks.* CIRCE *and* BRAVO *stare at the chair and at each other. Then* CIRCE *strides into the kitchenette.*]
I have tonight's menu, Ma'am: Southern Fried Chicken, rice, sweet potato pie —
CIRCE: Why, I declare, Mr...Uhh...that sounds exactly like the *Parade* Magazine Easter story about "The First Lady's Special Soul Food Recipes."
BRAVO: No, Ma'am —
CIRCE: "Why do you seek for the living among the dead?"...I *despise* Southern Fried Chicken, etc., Mr Joyce...Is this "The Atomic Café — We Deliver?"
BRAVO: No, Ma'am, but there's a whole list here: There's, uh, prime rib, and saddle of —
CIRCE: Excuse me, Mr Jones. I have to call the White House to talk to Mrs Heidt to find out why —
[*She starts for the telephone.* BRAVO *intervenes with the walkie-talkie.*]
BRAVO: We can patch it right through the radio, Ma'am — This is Bravo to Able, do you copy? We have a message here for the First Lady's Secretary. Do you copy?
WALKIE-TALKIE VOICE: We copy, Bravo. We copy. Go ahead.
BRAVO: You can go ahead, Ma'am. Just dictate to me. Able, we're ready here. Do you copy?
WALKIE-TALKIE VOICE: Copy, Bravo. We have the White

ACT ONE

House on the line.

    [CIRCE *reaches for* BRAVO*'s lapel.* BRAVO *backs away.*]

BRAVO: Please, Ma'am, I have to set up the contact.

    [CIRCE *stares, then opens her folder. Her little black book falls to the floor. Both stare at the book.* CIRCE *retrieves it.*]

CIRCE: Well...Tell Mrs Heidt that I'm sorry I had to leave without talking to her. Tell her that they didn't give me any notice. Tell her —

BRAVO: This is "Back-up" to "Base." Do you copy?

SECOND WALKIE-TALKIE: This is Base to Back-up. We copy. Go ahead, Back-up, we have Mrs Heidt right here.

CIRCE: Hello, Lynne?

    [CIRCE *tries to share the walkie-talkie with* BRAVO. *Subtly, he shuts her out.*]

BRAVO: I'm ready, Ma'am.

CIRCE: For what?

BRAVO: Dictation.

    [*Pause.*]

CIRCE: Lynne, can you hear me?... Oh, well, cancel the following appointments, please, Lynne.

    [*Now both talk at once.* BRAVO *races verbally to keep up with her rapid reading. Several times* CIRCE *tries again to establish direct contact with her secretary, who may or may not be on the line.*]

BRAVO: ⎱ ...Mrs Milton Garabedian, United Way. American
CIRCE: ⎰ Red Cross Service Award, Mrs Morton Gomberg. Spastic Children's Foundation Annual Tea Dance Donor Award Ceremony, Mrs Paul Archer. The Developmentally Disabled: Japan, Korea, South-East Asia Conference of Concerned Citizens, Mrs Conrad Gould —

    [CIRCE *and* BRAVO *talk at the same time. He*

keeps moving. Both manage to avoid direct conflict. The pressures build.]

CIRCE: Lynne? — May I please talk directly to my secretary, Mr —? May I talk to Mrs Heidt, please!

BRAVO: ⎫ Mrs Irving Arabian. The Big Brother Boat People
CIRCE: ⎬ Tenth Annual Medal. Mrs Richard de la Sexiexs. The Orphans of the Storm Presentation in the E.O.B. ...Ms Tina Grant and the Layettes —

CIRCE: I said that I would like...Lynne! "The Tiger is loose." Can you hear me? I said, "The Tiger is loose!"

> [BRAVO *takes the papers from* CIRCE's *hands, pivoting away and continuing to read alone.* CIRCE *calls out her code, "The tiger is loose," in vain.*]

BRAVO: Still reading. Do you copy?...Sickle Cell Christian Following, The Reverend and Mrs Clyde D. Washington —

CIRCE: ...is loose! Goddamnit! I've had no chance to say goodbye to anyone, for Christ's sake —

> [*She struggles for a fierce moment, then exits to the bedroom, slamming the door.* BRAVO *terminates the reading abruptly.*]

BRAVO: ...and any other appointments to be cancelled, until after February first. — Do you copy, Base?

SECOND WALKIE-TALKIE: We copy, Back-up.

FIRST WALKIE-TALKIE: This is "Tower" to Back-up and Base. Out.

> [BRAVO *steps silently to the fire. He takes the poker and puts the tip into the flames.* CIRCE *opens her bedroom door to re-enter and* BRAVO, *hearing her, pokes up the fire. He keeps his back to her.* CIRCE *picks up her papers and lifts the telephone.*]

CIRCE: Hello, get me Arnold Vernon at the New York

ACT ONE

Times bureau in Washington.

> [BRAVO *spins around.* CIRCE *laughs silently as she hangs up.*]

All circuits "busy at the moment." — Actually I couldn't get the switchboard.

BRAVO: No, Ma'am.

> [BRAVO *puts down the poker. The shadows are deeper now.* BRAVO *and* CIRCE *stand and stare at each other. In the silence we hear the clock tick loudly.* CIRCE *hums a snatch from a World War II song, "The Rose of Old San Antone." She lifts a boot to* BRAVO, *then the other.*]

CIRCE: [*quoting from "King Lear"*] "Pull it off, I say. Harder, Harder."

> [BRAVO *kneels at her feet. Then* CIRCE *begins to look noisily in various cabinets for something.*]

Who's stolen the vodka? ...What the hell's this? *Six* bottles of New York State wine?

BRAVO: Would you like to place your dinner order now, Ma'am? The kitchen is ready any time you —

CIRCE: Vodka straight! What is this wine doing here, Mr, Mr, ah, "Bravo," is that your code-name today? Would you like a glass? Ah, I don't seem to see the bottle opener, or any other sharp instruments, in here. If you could...

BRAVO: Yes, Ma'am.

> [*During her bravura monologue* CIRCE *changes tempo, pitch, rhythm and even regional accents with a consummate virtuosity.* BRAVO, *behind his reflecting glasses, betrays no reaction at all.*]

CIRCE: "Bravo." Bravo...Bravo and Circe. Do you know who Circe was, Bravo?

BRAVO: No, Ma'am.

CIRCE: Don't you just adore the code-names they use around here? This camp was called "Shangri-La" by FDR; Ike renamed it after his grandson, David; and it is soon to be dubbed, as you know, "Camp Victory!"... And it's "Able," "Baker," "Bravo," and "Charlie" for the Secret Service grunts and cannon fodder like you; and for the royalty, like me, "Circe". And "Priam" for the President; and "Odysseus" for our long-headed Secretary of State; Kissinger was always "Ajax" — could you die? And of course Al Haig was "Achilles," who pouted in his tent and then went mad...and Jack Kennedy was "Lancer," before they killed him...The story is that the SS, the Secret Service, produces the names at random from their ICARUS computer, but that's a crock, isn't it?

[BRAVO *stares at* CIRCE *from behind his mirrored black glasses, then makes a note in his black book.* CIRCE *sets the rocker rocking with a gesture.*]

BRAVO: That I do not know, Ma'am.
CIRCE: I see. *That,* you do not know...Well, no matter. Circe was the name of an old-timey Greek witch that just happens to be assigned to me. *Me,* the former "Miss LSU" — and closet cultural critic, whose totally innocent off-the-record (or off-the-wall, if you agree with my husband's media advisers), whose completely innocent comments to certain trusted friends have sent our hero, our husband, to the hustings out in the Horse Latitudes of the New Hampshire Primary. Hip-high in snow and ten points down in the polls, trying to explain away the First Lady's midnight calls to the New York *Times*, without coming right out and saying that she's suffering from delusions of "Deep Throat" and headed for a padded cell at St Elizabeth's.

ACT ONE

[CIRCE *laughs heartily.*]

BRAVO: Here you are, Ma'am.

CIRCE: Here's to you, brave Bravo. And to all you famous large-speared, rank-smashing men of the White House advanced guard.

BRAVO: The menu —

CIRCE: "Circe the witch without mercy." It's true — she did turn men into beasts, but...but for *love* she would turn the wolves and lions and pigs back into men. Only younger, cleaner, wiser, more, ah, beautiful... So, thank you, sir.

BRAVO: You're welcome.

CIRCE: Yes, Bravo, thank you for everything. I'll just call in on the white phone if I get hungry.

[*She moves to pick up the receiver.*]

BRAVO: Ma'am, we do have a security situation. You —

CIRCE: We do? Surely not another dead cat in the offing?...A "security situation," you say?

BRAVO: Yes, Ma'am. Orders are not to leave you alone...I'll stay here in the lodge until 2400 hours, and then —

CIRCE: 2400 — until midnight —

BRAVO: Yes, Ma'am. I'll just sit in the hall or —

CIRCE: I see. Around the clock "security?" And what is the nature of this "security problem?" Nothing was mentioned to me at the White House or on the helicopter by Colonel Wirtz.

BRAVO: No, Ma'am. It just came in. No details yet...uh, terrorism...

CIRCE: At Camp David?

BRAVO: Yes, Ma'am.

CIRCE: [*overlapping*] Against *me?*

BRAVO: Ma'am?

CIRCE: And the President?

BRAVO: I do not —

CIRCE: I see...Well, thank you, Bravo. In that case I believe

I will just freshen up a bit. Excuse me, and feel free to at least take off those reflecting glasses...after all, night *is* falling, isn't it?

[*She exits, winking broadly at him. Then* BRAVO *sneaks to the closed bedroom door to listen; next, he peers through a hidden spy-hole into the bedroom. After a moment he quickly moves away to stand in the shadows, writing in his black book. The sound of a Beethoven symphony can be heard playing from the bedroom.* CIRCE *opens the door and stands in the frame, coatless.*]

Will Beethoven bother you, Bravo? I mean, it doesn't make you want to reach for your gun, does it?... You reckon it was the terrorists who removed the vodka and replaced it with all that New York wine?

BRAVO: No, Ma'am.

CIRCE: No...Well, let's just have some in that case. Don't you just love this artillery shell lamp? — There, that's better. [*turns it off*] I believe the First Lady before me was a World War II buff. Have you noticed this red pillow-slip dedicated "To a Dear Mother," from Camp Polk, Louisiana, circa 1942? A stunning archeological artifact, isn't it? Ah, *nostalgie de la boue! Comprenez-vous?*

BRAVO: Ma'am?

CIRCE: I say we all long for mother, the primal slime, and to be born again, don't we?... Am I boring you, soldier?

BRAVO: No, Ma'am.

CIRCE: Do I detect a flicker of recognition behind those mirrored shades? You remember World War II, don't you, Bravo? — It was in all the papers...

Wine? Oh no, I forgot, we're on alert, aren't we?
BRAVO: No, thank you, Ma'am.
> [CIRCE *tours the room, touching objects, then leaps up on the couch and poses.*]

CIRCE: Do you adore "art deco?" — Doomsday chic, my dear... Umm. Camp Polk. *A la recherche du temps perdu.* "To a Dear Mother." Jesus, Camp Polk. You see, Bravo, that's where I was born — about ten miles away in a little old Southern town called Alexandria, Louisiana. Actually in Pineville, Louisiana, but that's where the asylum was so *we* always said Alexandria... And that's not far from Bienville Parish, where "they" shot Bonnie and Clyde into history. You've heard of —
BRAVO: Negative.
CIRCE: "Someday they'll go down together;
And they'll bury them side by side;
To few it'll be grief —
To the law a relief —
But it's death for Bonnie and Clyde."

Bonnie wrote that. She, ah...Hand me that bottle will you, Clyde? *Merci.* Where were we...ahh, yes, World War II.
> [*She drains her glass.*]

My daddy ran a soldiers' club during the war. "*The* Soldiers' Club!" And I used to see all the boys on the weekends when they'd come in from Camp Polk and Camp Lee, and Beauregard and Jackson — a million men poured through that little old town before I was ten years old. And they all came to my daddy's Soldiers' Club to buy red pillows with yellow fringes that said "To Sister," or "To Mother," or to anybody and everybody else in their extended clans back home in Dog Patch, or on the million-footed pavements of Metropolis... Do your security duties include pouring another glass of this high-class wine, soldier?

BRAVO: Yes, Ma'am.

CIRCE: Thank you, sir. Umm...World War II. Yes, indeed. Before your time. Way before, you can't be more than thirty, can you?

BRAVO: Thirty-three, Ma'am... Did you want me to order you a dinner from the — ?

CIRCE: No, Mr Bravo, I want to *drink*. Not eat, drink!... Where did you get *your* baptism of fire, Vietnam?

BRAVO: Yes, Ma'am.

CIRCE: Ummm. Not at all like World War II, was it?... Let's drink a Jax or a Regal to all the dog faces and shave tails and chicken colonels at all the camps and bases, shall we? And to all the God-fearing great patriots like my daddy, all the cockroach capitalists and Main Street boosters who made fortunes out of it all.

[*sings*] "Bless 'em all, bless 'em all,
The long and the short and the tall..."

...That was the Golden Age, Bravo. And you missed it, didn't you? ...The age of heroes. The gallant and golden lads of the Free World and the Four Freedoms who sailed away to fight fascism — You remember fascism, Bravo? Fascism came along somewhere after Protestantism and before Communism...I mean, how did all y'all golden lads become the B-Movie butchers of Teheran and Guatemala City and Saigon and Santiago — from the heroes of Grenada to the whores of Tripoli!

[*Suddenly* BRAVO *leaps and shouts "Down!" He hurls* CIRCE *headlong onto the couch then throws himself over her. He runs out through the door. Gun out.* CIRCE *goes for the kitchen wall telephone. It is dead, too. The helicopter roars overhead. Then, silence.* BRAVO *re-enters. The two stare at each other for a long moment in a ticking silence.*]

Just like you handled that dead cat... What I'm trying to tell you is that you can no longer tell who's a monster. There's just guys who look like, well, *you* — or me... There's no monsters any more, just arrow collar killers and clean-cut kids like you. That's what happened to all the golden lads from World War II. They *did* come home — as spooks, spies, unlaid ghosts, shades — like you, under cover of night, *comprende?*

BRAVO: No, Ma'am.

CIRCE: Ghosts. Revenants... What y'all call the "Body Count" and the Greeks named the "piteous dead"... Do those sunglasses screen out all the shadows, soldier?

BRAVO: Ma'am?

CIRCE: I'm saying that you're not really a "secret agent," Bravo...

[BRAVO *reacts by taking out his notebook.*]

I'm saying that you're a shade, an unlaid ghost. A ghost...Unlaid. Nothing personal...That's where "Circe" comes in, you see?

BRAVO: No —

CIRCE: Circe sent travelling men of war into hell. Down into Hades, into the Kingdom of the Dead. — Welcome to the White House, Bravo! And a young man — fast on his feet, like you — was her agent... You see, Circe was a witch who could love; and she had suffered, too, so she understood and gave the stranger guidance home, through the Kingdom of the Dead — and then they had a child, and the child —

>   [BRAVO *moves.*]
>   Code "Green." There's no one out there. There's nothing out there but sacred animals in the moonlight... Well, what do you think of my theory, Sergeant?
> BRAVO: I don't know —
> CIRCE: Take off your glasses when you address me, G-Man.
> BRAVO: I don't —
> CIRCE: How dare you stand there behind those black mirrors? How dare you put me under house arrest, you Xerox! — "Terrorists!" I smell a dead cat, you cipher. You have put me under around-the-clock surveillance so that, ostensibly, I can't get drunk and try to kill myself again, but, in reality, to *drive* me to it. I am going into my bedroom now, and if any of you SS creeps try to sneak in to see if I'm playing with myself or slashing my wrists or smuggling out a message to the New York *Times* or in any other way "embarrassing the White House" — I'll have your all-American *balls!*
>   [*She smashes the wine bottle on the sink and backs toward the bedroom, brandishing the jagged neck at* BRAVO. *As she backs out she sings —*]
>   "So we're saying goodbye to them all...
>   The long and the short and the tall..."
>   [CIRCE *exits.* BRAVO *picks up a piece of broken bottle. He begins, slowly, to close his hand over the glass as the winter light fades to black. In the dark we hear a helicopter dimly, off. After a moment we hear* BRAVO *speaking softly. A beam of moonlight slants up slowly through the window. There is a faint glow from the fireplace.*]

ACT ONE

BRAVO: Bravo to Able, Bravo to Able. 1800 hours. Circe is secure, repeat, Circe is asleep and secure. Do you copy?

> [*What sounds like an old black woman's voice is heard humming, off.*]

WALKIE-TALKIE VOICE: We copy, Bravo. Contact at 2000 hours. Out.

> [*The lights bump up.* CIRCE *stands in the doorway with her hand on the room lightswitch.*]

CIRCE: Irish coffee. Now! On the double.

> [BRAVO *moves toward the kitchenette.*]

I see that you respond to orders. Halt! Let's drop the double-speak, shall we? I mean, I won't play the First Lady and you just be — what is your first name?

BRAVO: Ma'am?

CIRCE: My old black mammy nicknamed me "Bootsie." Addie Mae Gatewood *née* Perry named me. That was before they...

> [*She does a vivid cameo of her old black mammy.*]

"Huh-uh! Now, child, I don't have to stay here. I can go to Chicago. I'm fixin' to go, child!"... I don't believe you'd've liked Addie Mae Gatewood *née* Perry...

> [*Silence, then fast and low:*]

You tight-lipped clone son-of-a-bitch! All right: You *be* Bravo, then, and I'll be Circe, and I'll give you blood to the horses' brow!... [*whispers*] Addie?

BRAVO: Ma'am?

CIRCE: How about making us some coffee? — No, I do *not* want food. Please, for Christ's sake, make me a cup of black coffee. Thank you... The last time I ate the food here I damn near died... Yes, you remember, over New Year's? My so-called sleeping pill suicide attempt carefully leaked to a few of our "elite assets" in the media. You know the type — sclerotic CIA groupies like Mr Rosencrantz of the *Times* and Mr Guildenstern of the *Post*.

[CIRCE *waves her black book at* BRAVO]

[*imitates Bogart*] By the way, sweetheart, don't bother tearing these priceless antiques apart looking for the "Maltese Falcon." This is my life insurance...or my death warrant, whatever. But it stays right here, where anybody can find it, along with the rest of my secrets.

[CIRCE *slips the book inside her blouse. The helicopter chops into hearing range.*]

Is that one helicopter or many?... Never mind, I have a pretty good idea of what they're up to and who they're coming for... If you don't call in on that squawk box that you've "secured" my little black book by a certain hour, then they send in the first team for search and destroy. — True?

[BRAVO *does not answer. The chopper retreats. The clock ticks.* CIRCE *puts on a recording of classical Spanish guitar. Only a pale wash of moonlight covers parts of the room. Music.*]

You like? It's the good news from the nervous system.

[CIRCE *begins a Spanish dance. She circles him. Then she comes to a halt, facing him.*]

...Standing there, shades drawn, looking like a punk-rock version of Hamlet..."Goodnight, sweet Prince."... You're staring, Bravo, behind your shades you're staring in amazement. And I'm sure they're blue, so blue, all you SS bravos have eyes that are so blue.

[BRAVO *goes to prepare instant coffee.*]

I've never taken a sleeping pill in my life! The news stories were a tissue... But I was so drunk, I get so drunk any more that I can't really fight back and remember what *did* happen. All I remember is... I was in here trying to get my hands on that sweet Mr Kercelik — the Polish SS boy with the corn-silk hair and the lethal blue eyes? All you boys are so fair, so golden — I think *his* code-name was "Bravo," too, or was it "Able?" I believe I questioned him rather closely as to whether or not he was able... How do you all have blue eyes? [*sotto voce*] "How do you like your blue-eyed boys now, Mr Death?"...

BRAVO: Cream?

CIRCE: No, thanks, plain. — Ugh. "New York Coffee." That's what they call it in New Orleans if you ask for coffee without chicory. [*imitating a waiter with a heavy New Orleans accent*] "Two cups of New York coffee..." Where are you from, Bravo? Just to chat about some other topic than who in the White House is trying to do me in, or alternatively, my terminal paranoia if you accept the official line... So, you were born and raised where? Whittier, California?

BRAVO: No, Ma'am. Rhinelander, Wisconsin.

CIRCE: Very good. Somehow I thought all you SS boys were from Whittier — Mr Nixon's home town. I don't know why. I just picture a gene-pool of pocket-sized, blue-eyed yahoos and used car salesmen in polyester suits and mirrored shades... Forgive me, Bravo, I'm not drunk and/or crazy, altogether, just a bit, ah, "nervous," as they used to say — and, of course, scared — so talk to me, soldier, about Wisconsin, the northwoods, the lake country... You're not my jackal, are you, Bravo?

[*There is a dead pause. The helicopter rockets in and out.* CIRCE *reacts.* BRAVO *makes an entry in his small black book.*]

I knew Martha Mitchell. Yes, I knew the lady. You don't have to be crazy to camp in the corridors of power but it helps, Bravo, it helps. But I'm not Martha. Oh, I'm a kind of a stand-up tragedian myself and under this flannel tongue some say that I, too, have a heart of gold *lamé*... Did you know the lady, Bravo?

BRAVO: No, Ma'am.

CIRCE: Am I your first First Lady?

BRAVO: Yes, Ma'am.

[CIRCE *looks at pictures*]

CIRCE: Well, you haven't missed much. There was Mamie on the sauce; then Camelot and *anorexia nervosa* or the "Beautiful People"; Pat Nixon with time on her hands in the Lincoln bed. And all the other poor molls in there with those gangsters...and "Great Men"... Do you think that's why the Founding Fathers caused the White House to be built in a swamp and the Congress up on "The Hill" — so that they could keep an eye on the Executive down there in the swamp?... I see you're not a student of history, Bravo, but it's true, you know. The Fathers feared us... I never touched a sleeping pill in my life!... Well, so...you grew up and died, where? Ah, yes, Rhinelander.

BRAVO: Yes, Ma'am.

CIRCE: ...And then? Talk to me or I'll kill myself... Or is that the plan?

BRAVO: When I was thirteen I went to the military academy in Delafield, Wisconsin.

CIRCE: ...And then?

BRAVO: I went to the State University at Oshkosh, Army ROTC.
CIRCE: ...Go on!
BRAVO: Graduated, went to Vietnam near the end...
CIRCE: Officer?
BRAVO: Sergeant.
CIRCE: Intelligence?
BRAVO: No, Ma'am, Special Forces.
CIRCE: Ahh, Green Beanie...
BRAVO: Yes, Ma'am.
CIRCE: Now we're getting somewhere. — Phoenix program?
BRAVO: Yes, Ma'am.
CIRCE: Torture and assassination?
BRAVO: Interrogation and —
CIRCE: Torture and assassination, Bravo!... I'm sorry. Here, have some of my coffee. You see, I trust you to make the coffee... But you have deceived, betrayed and murdered, haven't you, Bravo — many times in Vietnam?
BRAVO: We were at war.
CIRCE: In America, too?
BRAVO: We had to stop 'em somewhere.
CIRCE: Who? Where and why?
BRAVO: Them. Everywhere. To keep America free.

[CIRCE *tries to get through but* BRAVO *only writes in his black book.*]

CIRCE: America *is* free. The only problem is it's inhabited by a clutch of "Great Men." ...But I live in another country altogether, Bravo. You may have heard rumors of it — the United States? It's a place with real people — you know the type. But you live in America, don't you, with my husband and his abandoned ass-kissers? And America is the name of a nervous disease and an air-craft carrier. Put that in your little black book. We have a Statue of Liberty, too — and she's black — put that in too... No, but seriously — you might be a Russian and not an American. There's not a dime's worth of difference. Hmm? Well, if you are a KGB imposter, I leave you to your wax lover lying in wait for you in Red Square. You see, Bravo, the Soviets make their great men into mummies, and we, ah, do the opposite. Get it?

BRAVO: Negative.

[CIRCE *goes into the kitchenette singing "Born in the USA."*]

CIRCE: Here, test this cheese for me, will you?... "She waited a decent interval for the rat to die."...Ha ha! I once wanted to write, Bravo. You can probably tell — witty things like that. Here, have some, it's good... Ah, here you are guarding my bod from the madman of the month and I go and refuse to eat, and poor you has to choose between Velveeta and nothing. Oh, yes, I know the feeling. I choose Velveeta. Join me; it's permitted, we are "truly needy."

[BRAVO *is immobile.* CIRCE *holds out her hand, almost begging, with cheese in it.*]

BRAVO: Negative.

CIRCE: It's not poisoned is it? It's G.I. issue, the good kind that all the white trash, niggers and Mexicans line up for... If you don't take some, that means it *is* poisoned, and I'll —

[BRAVO *reaches out and takes a piece of cheese.* CIRCE *turns away.*]

I'm ravenous. Always. Is that good — or bad?

[*As she turns back she catches* BRAVO *throwing his cheese into the waste basket. She explodes.*

> *Slowly she strips the shelves and ice box — ripping, tearing, disposing of any and all edibles.*]

Thus spake Circe the witch:
Glut and swink, eat and drink,
Gobble food and guzzle wine.
Too vile, I say, for humankind
But quite right, I think, for *swine!*

> [CIRCE *"animalizes" her curse.*]

...And their noses grew wide and long. Their hair hardened into bristles, their hands and feet became hooves, and they ran about on all fours, snuffling and sobbing real tears from their little red eyes...

> [CIRCE *suddenly whispers hoarsely to* BRAVO, *pointing to the stuffed animals.*]

But all the pigs and stags and dogs of war knew that they were actually men — everybody knows, Bravo, what they've done and what's coming!

> [CIRCE *stalks to her bedroom, then returns with a quart of vodka, as* BRAVO *cleans up the mess.*]

And that's why the pigs all have sad little red eyes. But your eyes are big and blue, aren't they, Bravo?... The Martha Mitchell treatment. Here's to her: The town crier of Pompeii. She tried to tell the press that there were "bad things" in the White House, and they put her under house arrest in San Diego and shot her in the butt with psychotropic drugs and ripped the phones out of the wall and, for all I know, they killed her because she knew where the bodies were buried in the Rose Garden, and so do I, Bravo — so do I!... Private stock. Want some? It's safe. So you see, stud, I'm not a drunk and I'm not a whore. But I do know their dirty little nuclear secrets.

> [BRAVO *retreats into the dark kitchenette and*

begins a muttered colloquy on the walkie-talkie.
CIRCE *follows him.*]
That's when the White House started leaking — "She may have been 'Miss LSU' and a Phi Beta Kappa because she was putting out to all the Professors and T.A.'s —" And that's a big fat lie. Not *all* of them. — "But it's time the public knew that she had an abortion *and* a breakdown in Baton Rouge and was already a burned-out beauty queen at twenty when that millionaire young Congressman got into her knickers during Mardi Gras after the Comus parade. Though they do say she snuck into his suite at the Roosevelt and then tricked him into marrying her — the witch — and sunk her talons into his Brooks Brothers coat-tails and rode the poor department store dummy all the way to the White House. Oh yes, she's a dipsomaniacal nymphomaniac — according to one high souse, hic, source — and a nymphomaniacal dipsomaniac, according to another." ... These selective leaks *have* reached your pointed little pig ears, haven't they, Sergeant?

BRAVO: No 'm.

[CIRCE *is suddenly vulnerable.*]

CIRCE: Thank you... So much for your ears. Now, we come to your eyes. Are those glasses regulation, even inside, even at night?

BRAVO: Optional.

CIRCE: You're not the blind —

BRAVO: No, Ma'am —

CIRCE: — leading the blind?

BRAVO: No, Ma'am.

CIRCE: ...Please take them off. I won't tell anyone...

[BRAVO *takes out his notebook and begins to jot*

> *notes of some kind.* CIRCE *tries to look;* BRAVO *swivels away. Again, she tries to make contact.*]

...Do you play chess, Bravo?

BRAVO: No, Ma'am.

CIRCE: No...Would you like me to read Nietzsche or something else light to you? And music by Wagner? Wait.

> [CIRCE *blows dust from a book and puts on "Tristan and Isolde."*]

Hmm..."Does not nature keep things secret, even about the body? ... And man, indifferent to his own ignorance, is resting on the pitiless, the greedy, the insatiable, the murderous — hanging, as it were, hanging in dreams on the back of a tiger."... What do you think? That's this gang, isn't it, hanging in dreams on the back of a tiger?... And the tiger is loose, isn't it, Bravo?

BRAVO: Beg pardon?

CIRCE: The deep thinkers and the Gods of War with the brass balls around here that you guard, do you think that they have the faintest idea of what's going on? When the President made that slip of the tongue at his year-end press conference, didn't that tell you something?

BRAVO: I'm not —

CIRCE: When he slipped and referred to the integrity of the Joint "Cheats" — C-H-E-A-T-S — instead of Joint *Chiefs*. When he said that according to the Cheats and their "Team B Report" that the Russians are coming —

BRAVO: No, Ma'am.

CIRCE: No...Well, shall we continue? "Beware that when you look into the abyss that it doesn't look into you —"

BRAVO: Negative.
CIRCE: Not your cup of tea? I thought you might be a Superman fan.
BRAVO: No, Ma'am.
CIRCE: Check. — What are you — Lutheran? You know your "Song of Solomon"?
BRAVO: Negative.
CIRCE: "...I am a wall and my breasts are like towers...for love is as strong as death"... You remember "love", don't you, Bravo — the pursuit of politics by other means. — No?... Well, if we're stuck together here until midnight let's do *something* together. Chess? No, that's right. Pinochle?
BRAVO: No 'm.
CIRCE: Shall I try to guess who you are and where you —?
BRAVO: No 'm.
CIRCE: Are you aware that all you've really said to me is "No?"
BRAVO: I'm —
CIRCE: — only following orders?
BRAVO: Yes, Ma'am.
CIRCE: I see...Ahh, well... Strip poker? No, all that machine-tooled perfection might unhinge me... Riddles — you like riddles?
BRAVO: Negative.
CIRCE: The opposite of love is — what? I *order* you to answer.
BRAVO: Hate.
CIRCE: And the opposite of war is —?
BRAVO: Peace.
CIRCE: Wrong. You're wrong, Mr *Right*. The opposite of love is fear. And the opposite of war is not peace — it's love... Last chance, now: the opposite of peace is...?
BRAVO: War.

ACT ONE

CIRCE: No. Power... War is the opposite of justice. And desire is the opposite of death... What shall we play now?...

> [CIRCE *paces like a tiger.*]

[*suddenly*] Karate!

> [CIRCE *attacks* BRAVO. *He is forced to leap away and retreat, countering. She is fierce and balletic, giving voice to horrific shouts and sound effects. They circle the room in serious engagement. Finally* BRAVO *kicks a warning, shouts, and then seizes* CIRCE'S *wrists. They stand panting and staring at each other. He lets her go.*]

"You're good, you're very good," as they used to say in the movies... I know — we'll play "White House." No tricks, I promise. Just follow me. — Come on. Bet I can make you laugh. — Smile?

> [BRAVO *follows her with his eyes only.* CIRCE *pretends to conduct a guest on a tour of the White House. She acts out the travesty in broad camp, clambering over furniture, changing voices, etc.*]

C'mon! Now here, of course, we have the Blue Room — where the living envy the dead — so named in honor of the terminal depression of your average First Lady — [*sings*] "Am I blue...?" Now, here, for instance, is the Reagan antimacassar display. And this is the new wallpaper — "Either that wallpaper goes or I do," I laughingly told the President. Guess what he replied? ... Where are we? Ah, yes, the downstairs linen closet... It is in these laundered confines that a long-since-forgotten Vice-President, wrapped only in a flag, collapsed and expired in the corky arms of the President's boxing instructor, who had, only the day before, taken the Vice-President's wife and spinster daughter, by turns, in this same cozy hideout. The White House, sir, has served proudly, as a sort of national whorehouse. Here we *do* see the moral equivalent of war — necrophilia! And the series of mad-women we jokingly call the First Ladies have had to preside over it all. My God, you can still hear their screams and sobs from the Hoover bedroom on steamy Potomac nights. Now, just in here is the upstairs sitting-room — where, you may remember, Mr Nixon and Dr Kissinger knelt on this Persian rug — a gift from the Shah himself — and prayed to their God that he might loose the hounds of the Watergate and smite flat the packs of the press! And this is the Coolidge Lounge, where a final "photo opportunity" captured for all time a tearful Mr Nixon bidding a fond farewell to a White House staff splitting its faces with enormous grins…

[CIRCE *snaps her fingers. She launches a new plan of action.*]

Wake up! I'm asking questions to make sure that you're the real Bravo. You've "surveilled" and secured every room in the White House, haven't you?

BRAVO: Yes, Ma'am.

CIRCE: And you know the history of the place, don't you?… They teach you that where?

BRAVO: Protective Reaction Group Special Forces Study.

CIRCE: Right. And where is that located?

BRAVO: Near the old farm out in —

CIRCE: The code-name for the black brief-case chained to the wrist of the agent who follows the President everywhere?

BRAVO: Negative.

CIRCE: The code-name for the brief-case with the button inside? The doomsday machine with the crazy computer chip waiting to be pushed by one of those "Great Thinkers" who —

BRAVO: "Football."

CIRCE: "*Football.*" Correct! And the agent's code-name?
 [*She throws the "mother" pillow to* BRAVO]

BRAVO: "Line-backer."

CIRCE: Right again. By what name did Presidents Monroe, Fillmore, Coolidge, Reagan — and as many as a dozen others — what name, or how did they address their wives?

BRAVO: Mother or Mommy.
 [*He stares at the pillow.*]

CIRCE: You're the "right stuff," all right... Listen! They told you I was some kind of sexual turnstile that y'all had to go through, *seriatim*, on the road to advancement. Is that it?
 [CIRCE *is addressing* BRAVO *with vulnerable openness now.*]

BRAVO: No —
 [*He puts the pillow down.*]

CIRCE: Listen, Bravo, sex is like torture: it fills up the world... You know about torture?

BRAVO: Yes, Ma'am.

CIRCE: Wait. Listen. You know the Carlton painting in the Lincoln Bedroom?

BRAVO: "Waiting for the Hour."

CIRCE: Yes. And the content of the picture?

BRAVO: Slaves waiting for midnight, December 31, 1862. Waiting for their hour of freedom...

CIRCE: That's the only important painting in all that wilderness of Steamboat-Gothic junk and memorabilia... Is it possible, Bravo, that you and I are both waiting for that hour?...

[*She is almost ready to break. She waits in vain for a sign from* BRAVO.]

Not an inch, huh? Oh, well… "Under the spreading cherry tree — I sold you and you sold me"…
[*Pause.*]
Oh God! Talk to me. Tell me the history of something — anything — the Vermeil Room.

BRAVO: …And this is the Vermeil Room.
[CIRCE *stares at* BRAVO.]
Sometimes called the Gold Room.

CIRCE: …Go on.

BRAVO: …It was completely refurbished in 1971 and serves now as a display room and ladies' sitting-room.
[*Pause.*]

CIRCE: That's it, Sergeant — go on.

BRAVO: The panelled walls have been painted a soft green to complement the collection of vermeil, or gilded silver —

CIRCE: Perfect, Private! Go on —

BRAVO: — bequeathed to the White House in 1956 by Mrs —

CIRCE: Correct, Cadet! Keep going!

BRAVO: — Margaret Thompson Biddle. In 1817 —
[CIRCE *gambles that she can push* BRAVO *back into an earlier, more vulnerable stage of his life.* BRAVO *stumbles after her, seeming to respond.*]

CIRCE: Speak up, Cadet, I can't hear you! Come here, you scrawny, homesick human pimple. Get in here, "new boy," *now*!
[BRAVO *recites in a sad young voice.*]

BRAVO: Sir, scamp new boy out, sir.
Sir, scamp new boy out, sir.
Sir, scamp new boy out, sir.

CIRCE: Marvelous…Oh, ah, come in, new boy…stand up

straight, you cretin. You're a beastly cretin, aren't you?

BRAVO: Yes, sir.

[CIRCE *circles the "new boy," picking at him.*]

CIRCE: Speak up, cretin — is there mush in your mouth?

BRAVO: Yes, sir.

CIRCE: Well, mush mouth?

BRAVO: Permission to expectorate, sir?

CIRCE: Has it got "bones" in it?

BRAVO: Yes, sir.

CIRCE: Then swallow it!

[CIRCE *touches him on the pretext of inspecting his uniform.*]

Right face. Right face. About face. Present "arms." The definition of Power?

BRAVO: Power: Sir, Power is the ability to make other people act against their own interests, sir.

CIRCE: And?

BRAVO: And Power is the Power to hurt those without Power, sir.

CIRCE: Perfect. The school motto!

BRAVO: "Death before Dishonor."

CIRCE: The school song?

BRAVO: [*in a lonely, young voice*]

"And there was Captain Washington,
 Upon a strapping stallion,
And giving orders to his men,
 I guess there was a million."

CIRCE: "Yankee Doodle keep it up,
 Yankee Doodle dandy,
Mind the music and the step
 And with the girls be handy."

Stand up! Suck it in, get a haircut. Now, speak up, you robot, recite the Order of Battle.

BRAVO: Yes, sir: In World War I the side with the cleanest trenches won the battle, sir. In World War II the Chiefs-of-Staff favored letting Germany and Russia destroy each other, sir. In World War III there *will* be survivors, sir. According to President Truman, God gave America the Atomic Bomb —

CIRCE: Stop! At ease. Let go. Things run down —

BRAVO: Second Law of Thermodynamics!

CIRCE: Shut up! I want your order of the day, as of *today*. This morning. You understand?

BRAVO: Yes, sir.

CIRCE: White House Briefing Room, 0800 hours, Colonel Wirtz speaking. Repeat his orders.

BRAVO: [*with a Texas twang*] You men listen up. We're on "Go" today...

CIRCE: What's that mean?

BRAVO: I'm gonna tell you boys one time — I don't want that little lady to leave that lodge, you hear?...

CIRCE: What else? — Anything else?

BRAVO: Negative.

CIRCE: All right. Uh, ah, 1500 hours. You're here in the compound, at "Base." Who's there with you?

BRAVO: Able and Charlie.

CIRCE: And what do they say?

WALKIE-TALKIE VOICE: Bravo, report to Tower. Over.

BRAVO: [*in a Boston accent*] Wait till she's drunk to —

CIRCE: To what? *What?*

BRAVO: I don't know, sir.

WALKIE-TALKIE VOICE: Bravo, report to Tower. Over.

[BRAVO *exits.* CIRCE *tries the telephone again. She is so bruised that she continues to talk to herself, into the dead phone.*]

CIRCE: I know you can hear me...I need help...I need Addie, I need Addie Mae Gatewood to help me, now before it's too late...

[*She sees* BRAVO *staring at her through the porch window. She tries to cover her dread by resuming the "Grand Tour."*]

...And last of all we have this ulterior decorator's remodelled Howard Hughes picture window looking out on a blank wall. — And I'm up against it.

[CIRCE *is against the wall.* BRAVO *re-enters. For a moment,* CIRCE *resumes her play-acting, then sings a snatch of Brecht-Weill, leaping onto the coffee table, sounding like Marilyn Monroe.*]

But it's show business, right, Bravo? It's all lies and they don't really make love in secret or any other way in that whited sepulchre — they make *war*. They play with themselves and make war in secret; they gang-bang our people and they make war!... It's tits and ass, Bravo. We're all "stars," and the "masses" are supposed to spread their legs in mob scenes of adoration. It's spectacle, Bravo; the circus for Nero... Show business. Theatre! As in "Theatre Nuclear War." "Light 'em up, boys, dah de de dah. Happy endings are the rule..."

[*She remains on the table.*]

You think I can't stop talking, don't you?

BRAVO: No, Ma'am.

CIRCE: You better pray that I don't. There are worse torments, believe me, than my logorrhea and mythomania.

[BRAVO *continues to write in his black book.*]

Listen, football boy, I have a message from the coach for you... Someone is coming to take the ball out of the hands of the terrible players... So don't wait until the clock runs out and the final gun goes off...[*whispers*] ... You reckon that I'm down and out now, don't you? That it's only a matter of hours before I'm boxed out of my mind and then I'll jump

or you can push me? But you are in for the shock of
your life. You see, Kilroy, I am not alone.

BRAVO: Excuse me, Ma'am.

CIRCE: Here, look...you know about "Mutual Assured
Destruction," "MAD" — but look at this "Nuclear
Utilization Theatre Selection"..."Nuts!"

> [*Reading from her little black book,* CIRCE
> *pleads with* BRAVO, *but he exits.*]

Mad!... Opium stockpiles hidden in all major
hospitals"..."Mass suicide ordered in case of..."
Wait — "Dioxin in mother's milk denied — cancer
cost acceptable..."Look — "Negotiations to commence
after a hundred million..." "Change-of-
address cards at post offices to comfort public when
—" [*laughing and crying in torment*] "Bomb freeways
to open up the —" [*screams*] Nuts!

> [*She runs out through the lodge door. A
> helicopter cuts her off. We hear the chopping,
> siren sounds. A loudspeaker voice from the
> chopper booms through the compound:* "Bravo,
> do you copy? Bravo, where are you? Do you
> copy?..." *Another voice:* "Get that woman out of
> there!" *etc.* CIRCE *races back in, into her
> bedroom and slams the door.* BRAVO *is just
> behind her. The chopper cuts out and suddenly
> we hear two voices from inside* CIRCE's *bedroom.
> At this,* BRAVO *draws his revolver and tries to
> contact* "Tower" *by walkie-talkie. The two
> voices are those of* CIRCE *as an adolescent and of
> a dynamic and older black woman, Addie Mae
> Gatewood.*]

"ADDIE": [*off*] Bootsie, child, what they doin' to you?

CIRCE: [*off*] Addie, they want to kill me or make me go
crazy so they can carry me to the 'sylum and give
me 'lectric shock the way they did you that time —

[*The door flies open and* BRAVO *is confronted by* CIRCE *as* ADDIE MAE GATEWOOD. CIRCE *has transformed herself physically and vocally into a lean sixty-year-old black woman of such electric energy and galvanic force that even* BRAVO *is shaken. She picks up a cane from the coat-stand and brandishes it.*]

"ADDIE": White boy! Don't say a word. I'm gonna cut you if you stand still and shoot you if you run. You the one been messin' with my Bootsie? Answer me, you thin-lipped trash!

BRAVO: I —

"ADDIE": I know you! You the one tried to tie me up and carry me to the 'sylum in Pineville, ain't you?

[*She advances on* BRAVO. *He feints and dodges.*]

BRAVO: This is Bravo to Tower —

"ADDIE": Put that whatchamacallit down, you dog. Your wife, she cheated me about those pecans and I told her it was a shame and a sin to cheat poor people the way y'all do. If I ever catch you near my little girl again, I'm going to send you to your maker, you hear me? You hear me good, white boy? — I'm comin', honey... Do it hurt, baby?

[*She backs out and slams her bedroom door. In the silence, then, we hear* "ADDIE" *speak and sing.*]

"ADDIE": [*off*] Do it hurt, baby? Mm, Mm. Deed it do. Yes, Jesus, I know.

"Go down old Hannah.
And don't you rise no more
And if you rises in the morning
Bring Judgement Day."

[CIRCE *re-enters. She seems transformed.*]

CIRCE: They took her away one rainy evening...But she's always with me. So I am intact. Yes, child, they took

Addie Mae Gatewood *née* Perry off to Pineville and put her *under* the ground, the way I am now. Because Addie was a witch and a wizard who taught me what every woman who's ever survived has had to learn: how to be a *woman* — which is another name for a mental case — and yet not *act* like one, lest they come for you one day and carry you off to Pineville, or St Elizabeth's or that famous rest resort known as Camp David... You married? Children?

BRAVO: No, Ma'am.

CIRCE: Me either. And *I'm* sure... I need a child, soldier; a female child so that I can pass on the Eleusinian mystery from Addie. You understand?... You put your gun and your radio up and I'll tell you what I'll do — I'll go one on one with you. You can have it "sweet or salty," as Addie would have said — I'll fuck you or I'll fight you. But just you and me, no G-men riding to the rescue. — Come on, you want me at your throat or at your feet?

[*Moonlight and Wagner.*]

But who I really am is Circe, Bravo, granddaughter of Helios, the sun-God; daughter of Persë, who was the child of wild Oceanus. I can read dreams and make prophecy. I, too, can follow the blood-red footprints in the dark from Dallas to the Watergate. All the White House horrors. I, too, can hear the power glands of the "Great Men": pumping — pumping — pumping... But let us not speak of me, but of you, stranger. You are an adventurer, a man of the sword, a hawk of the sea. You have come through sad, sore times and now seek a haven here on my western isle. Welcome. I will protect and watch over you even as a mother cares for her worn-out son. I will shield you, wanderer, from the long foot of Time.

> [*Her voice is rich, seductive, hypnotic.* BRAVO *stares through his black glasses.* CIRCE *drapes a wolf-skin over* BRAVO.]

I will refresh you. I will have baths, perfumed baths, drawn for you, to wash you clean, clean of crime… Honey and cheese in red bowls shall slake all thirst and sate all hunger.

> [CIRCE *opens her robe and cups a breast, offering it to* BRAVO. *He is in a beam of moonlight as if mesmerized.*]

Eat, drink. Do not hold back your hunger. Give in, Bravo, *become* your hunger. Take the milk and honey from these timeless bowls of white and red…

> [*The two are in a moonlit tableau. The beam fades on their unresolved confrontation as, over the music, suddenly, the helicopter registers in the distance, coming closer.*]

END OF ACT ONE

ACT TWO

The sound of a slave song being sung in the dark by CIRCE. *It is now night but the action is continuous.* CIRCE *and* BRAVO *face each other as at the end of Act One.* CIRCE *sings "Go Down Old Hannah." The light is from the fire and the moon.* BRAVO *makes an entry in his black book.* CIRCE *is in her robe, singing against the helicopter sound.*

CIRCE: "...Should of been on the river,
    nineteen and ten
They was driving the women
    just like they do the men.

Go down, old Hannah
    and don't you rise no more
And if you rises in the morning
    set this world on fire."
    [*Silence.*]
— So the President's wife made a pass at you! Big deal. Don't take it personally, Blind Cupid... I'm starving... I trust you're equally shocked when you're assigned to guard that Air Force One circus of whoremasters on their junkets from Peoria to Peking? — Don't play the ass-aching Puritan with me, padre. You travelled with the President's party to California last summer, didn't you?

BRAVO: Yes, Ma'am.

CIRCE: Damn right. And you went with them to their secret men's camp in the Redwoods, didn't — ?

BRAVO: Yes, Ma'am —

CIRCE: Yes, Ma'am. "The Primeval Woods." And they brought the whores in helicopter hecatombs from

San Francisco, didn't they?...Didn't they? I know all about it, I have my agents, too, you know. They put y'all SS studs in their ritual entertainments, don't they?
BRAVO: Yes.
CIRCE: I know they do. Let's hear you recite your lines.
BRAVO: I —
CIRCE: That's an order... I've noticed, you always follow orders, in your own weird fashion. Speak to me of the "Rites of Pan," Stranger! C'mon. "... But fire will have its will with thee. And all the winds make merry with thy dust. Bring fire!"
BRAVO: "Cremation of Care, Cast your Griefs to fires
All who dare, quench now your secret desires."
CIRCE: What are your "secret desires," Bravo, and why don't you want to quench them?
   [*From the compound the sound of a crossed connection: "We have a guard dog down — we have a guard dog down."* CIRCE *runs to the window, stares out, then moves to a deeper level of communication.*]
I know all their secrets. Tell me, if you dare, the code-names of the two bombs, planned in the Primeval Woods, that they — *we* — dropped on Japan.
   [*Pause.*]
BRAVO: "Little Boy" and "Fat Man."
CIRCE: You got it. "Fat Man" — with Rita Hayworth painted on the side. But what you don't know is that in the 1940s, when they hid out there to plot how they would drop "Little Boy" and "Fat Man," then Oppenheimer and all the toughs of the Liberal Left decided that the bombs — both of them — had to be dropped on real, unsuspecting *people*. And I know why, because I've seen the documents!

Because, Bravo, they were all afraid, terrified, that the bomb might not work if they announced a demonstration; that they might not be able to get it up! "Fat Man" *manqué*, understand?... When the bomb worked at Los Alamos, a message was flashed to Berkeley: "It's a boy!" — You didn't know that, did you, Kilroy?

BRAVO: No 'm.

CIRCE: It's a boy... What's a "boy?" Hmm? Eloquent silence. Still, priest-warrior that you are, you must have noticed the drill for bringing in the whores up at good old "Primeval Woods," where the Wise Men, the Fathers of the Bomb, gather for their annual blood rites. The drill, Jock — the *whores!*

BRAVO: They dress them in cowboy boots and Eisenhower jackets and keep them in the south holding pen until they're needed.

CIRCE: The liverish skin, the purple war wounds — radioactive in the bonfire light — is that what turns you on, boy? The whores crawling like dogs on their hands and knees. And then all you boys, old and new, stop pissing on the timeless trees and — what is it that y'all do, Bravo? You and all your Christian he-men and power-broker rough trade, all those —

BRAVO: Nothing.

CIRCE: *Nada?* Are you telling me that these "Great Men" and heroic child molesters, late of World War II, permit you to bow out of their idyllic gang-bang?

BRAVO: Yes.

CIRCE: But you *are*, or were, a gang-banger, weren't you?

BRAVO: Negative.

CIRCE: In military school? With the town girls —

BRAVO: Negative.

CIRCE: Well...in Nam, then?

BRAVO: No —
CIRCE: Don't bullshit me, Bravo. You were up in I Corps, weren't you?
BRAVO: Yes, Ma'am.
CIRCE: And you "Greenies" gang-banged those "gooks," didn't you? In the huts, in the rice paddies, in the rain forests —
BRAVO: No!
CIRCE: I know all about it. And, believe it or not, it may be, in part, the most human thing y'all ever did over there. You see, Kilroy, what you all did to those heart-breakingly beautiful "slopes," y'all did to me a long time ago in the bayou country... You or country boys just like you. So you can remember, boy; you can tell me, because I've been there, and I know why you all do it that-a-way... Can you remember, country boy?

[BRAVO *is affected, against his will.*]

BRAVO: No.
CIRCE: You can't fool me, Bravo. Weren't you with Sonny Harris and Leonard Kaplan and them, that night after play practice?
BRAVO: What?
CIRCE: It was dark but I saw your face in the headlights. You were the new boy in town, the thousand-year-old new boy in town. And you had heard about me, hadn't you?
BRAVO: No, Ma'am, I've never —

[CIRCE *draws him into her memory.*]

CIRCE: Yes, you had. You knew that I never did belong to what we called the "400" in high school. And that was because I was letting Red Jordan and those football boys mess with me — in the cheerleaders' section of the bus — on out-of-town games. But I think a gang-bang is somehow more, ah, chaste, don't you, Bravo? I mean it's dark, you're on the back seat of the bus or out past the asylum in somebody's daddy's big old Cadillac, and you football boys are slipping in and out of the car as silent as ghosts. Holding up your rubber for me to see, like good little boys, and then "Hey, Bootsie, put it in for me, will ya?"... You remember that night, new boy?

>[BRAVO *is almost caught in her fugue and must wrench himself out.* CIRCE *lies back with a sobbing laugh.*]

BRAVO: No, Ma'am.

CIRCE: Do you *have* a memory, Bravo? Or have you come to the conclusion that because the past no longer exists that the organ known as the memory is just one more useless appendage like the heart or the soul? I think that's what you football boys, like my husband, all think... God, you look just like him twenty years ago... Where were we? The rubbers. The gang-bang boys would hold up their Ramses...or their...Trojans...Are you a Trojan, Bravo?

BRAVO: Ma'am?

CIRCE: A Trojan man, are you a Trojan, are you a horseback-breaking Trojan man?... Ah, well, it's all ancient Greek to you, isn't it?... Sheiks and Trojans and...

>[*She breaks for the front door as if to escape.*]

BRAVO: No! You can't —

CIRCE: Can't what, Bravo? Can't run home again?

BRAVO: No, Ma'am. My orders —

CIRCE: Your orders? "Operation Cassandra" — is that what you're telling me? Goddamnit! I'm talking about Martha — Martha Mitchell, and you know it!... What time is it?

BRAVO: 2241 hours. 10:41 p. —
CIRCE: 11:58, you say? That's funny, I have 11:59... Where were we? You recall?
BRAVO: No, Ma'am.
CIRCE: No...oh, but I do. Sit down, Rambo, give it a rest...
> [*She takes* BRAVO's *arm and forces him to sit with her on the couch.*]

We were in a big old Cadillac — or was it a Packard? — parked on a red clay road, 'bout a mile south of Pineville... I could see a sky full of stars from where I lay on the back seat, out through the rear window. And outside the car, whistling in the dark, I could hear all y'all football boys trying to get up your courage — you understand, Boy?
> [CIRCE *has him again. She whistles.*]

BRAVO: No 'm.
CIRCE: Yes you do. You country boys wanted me to change you from animals into human beings. You wanted to change your luck, didn't you? I was your rite of passage, that's all. Then you wouldn't have to get drunk and half kill each other in order to *touch* and be close. You had *me*. — And we won the state championship three years running, remember? But, see, Bravo, that "400" crowd detested me because not only had I become a religious symbol to the football team — I made the coach get down on his knees and beg for it — but I was already winning all kinds of little old beauty contests *and* I never fell below a straight A average until my last year, when I refused to give Mr Autrey any and the old fart gave me a B in chemistry... I'll tell you my first time if you tell me yours, O.K.?... Remember Buck Gremillion? Well, one night we were at the Rex watching John Wayne and I put my hand inside his popcorn box and what do you reckon was in there?

BRAVO: I don't know.
CIRCE: Guess...Guess!
BRAVO: His...phallus.
CIRCE: Ah, I see you *do* speak Greek. Well, child, my hand froze. — Completely. In a kind of permanent digital double-take... Then, it was Buck's turn to go into shock when I started in to squeeze. You see, he'd counted on me jumping away like I'd touched a red hot poker — and I would've if I could've — but instead my, ah, "nature" took over and that quite "unmanned" old Buck... Four days later he went into the priesthood. I never saw him again... It was so sad, Bravo, the way all that proud tumescence just fell in on itself...

> [*At the mention of a hot poker,* BRAVO *gives an involuntary shudder which* CIRCE *sees.* CIRCE *stretches on the couch in the moonlight.*]

And that's the "Primeval Woods Men's Retreat," isn't it? The "Nervous Nellies," the "pitiful giants" — but underneath the masculine protest and the body armor and all the tough talk about "standing tall," and the bulging rhetoric — underneath, they're as cold and small and scared as Buck was in his pubertal popcorn box... Ah, Bravo, the poor boys, the "piteous dead," those pathetic bundles of secrets, the poor, mad boys who're "soft on" fascism and who can't keep it up...

> [*She moves closer to* BRAVO *and begins to speak with absolute empathy. Over his head she revolves the pillow, "To Mother," hypnotizing him. Her tone is soft, but inexorable. Slowly she drives him to react, but never raises her voice, only tightening the emotional screws of their rapport.*]

How did you lose your cherry, Bravo?

BRAVO: Negative.
CIRCE: Tell me about your first time? I told *you*.
BRAVO: I can't remember.
CIRCE: Can't... Do you have a girl, Bravo?
BRAVO: Negative.
CIRCE: Why not?
BRAVO: No time.
CIRCE: No time, out of time? Me too... What do you do for, ah, relief?
BRAVO: Nothing.
CIRCE: Do you dream about it?
BRAVO: No 'm.
CIRCE: At military school. Cold nights, rough blankets, Vaseline...Christ, you're only human.
BRAVO: No, Ma'am.
CIRCE: Tell me your dreams...Everybody dreams, Bravo, or they go mad.
BRAVO: No 'm, not me.
CIRCE: Bravo, if you tell me your nightmare — we all have a nightmare — I'll tell you mine.
BRAVO: Negative.
CIRCE: All right, then, *I'll* tell you your nightmare.
BRAVO: Please —
CIRCE: Do?
BRAVO: Don't.
CIRCE: Why not, country boy?
BRAVO: Do you have the "need to?" —
  [*All overlapping; softly, subjectively:*]
CIRCE: Know? Yes, indeed, I need to know. We all —
BRAVO: "Need to know" —
CIRCE: You need to know that it's time to go home?
BRAVO: No 'm.
CIRCE: Home.
BRAVO: No 'm.
CIRCE: [*whispering*] Home.

BRAVO: Home...
CIRCE: Yes. I have it all written down in my little black book, home boy. It says here that a certain young Wisconsin football boy was wandering down a long...where? Is he going fishing or hunting? Is he outside or inside?
> [*A star pause. This is her last card to play. Then, out of the ticking, and through closed lips...*]

BRAVO: ...Inside.
CIRCE: Inside!
BRAVO: No!
CIRCE: Yes!...Inside. Inside the farmhouse or the...
> [CIRCE*'s genius is now to pick up the smallest verbal or silent clue until she can feel her way into* BRAVO*'s nightmare.* BRAVO *is mute again until, at last, a voice from far away, through locked lips, is barely audible.*]

BRAVO: The White House...
CIRCE: The White House?
BRAVO: Up the back stairs into the West Wing.
CIRCE: The Family Wing?
BRAVO: The Family Wing...
CIRCE: I know. I'm locked in there.
> [BRAVO *gropes as if in a dream.* CIRCE *stays with him. They remain facing forward.*]

BRAVO: They're locked — All the doors on the left are locked...
CIRCE: No, here's one on the right that opens. Quick, hide in here.
> [BRAVO *stands trembling violently.* CIRCE *holds on to him.*]

BRAVO: No, Ma'am, please...
CIRCE: I'll go with you, Bravo...
BRAVO: Not in there...

CIRCE: Let's go together, Blue-Sky Boy... I know that nightmare — the President wakes up every night screaming with that nightmare. C'mon — Through the White House...Through the farmhouse... Through Mother's room...Free!

BRAVO: Nooo!

[BRAVO *runs to the fireplace and plunges the hot poker into his hand. He falls, unconscious onto the couch. Slowly, in mortal conflict,* CIRCE *removes* BRAVO'*s dark glasses. She kneels to stare at him.* BRAVO *opens his eyes, then hands* CIRCE *his black book.*]

CIRCE: What language is this? Is this code? — Who are you?

[BRAVO *sits up slowly, talking simply to* CIRCE. *She is first amazed then stricken at this re-birth.* BRAVO'*s eyes can now be seen for the first time.*]

BRAVO: oh halane cha jai ca cushiba wa to toon we've got a dead man here dead man here zen ku stu dachi gedan bari oi tsuki able mmmmmmmmmm mmmmmmmmm mmmmmmmmmmm company able company quatzycotl med vac med vac jimp jingo shitstorm coming charlie at one o'clock black noise tare sha bocu ohu i have wounded i have wounded i have nai dad chee sow ohu nai dad shitstorm coming bovine vortex dead dog torpid ahhhh ahhhhh ahhhhh sequetor sequetor sequetor sequetor mama mmmmmmmmmmm mmmmmmmmmmm mmmmmmmmmmm now i lay me down to down to mama ak forty seven bouncing betties fruitcup cartel blood thump necrobiosis keep the field jihad someone coming my lai my lai khe san someones cominnng someones cominnng

[CIRCE *wipes a tear from* BRAVO'*s cheek, then*

sings and speaks, half ADDIE MAE GATEWOOD, *half herself.*]

CIRCE: "Thou art weak, but I am strong —
Jesus keep us from all harm."

Addie ain't gon' let 'em carry you to Pineville. Ain't gon' give you no 'lectric shock.

[CIRCE *helps* BRAVO *to rise so that she can dance with him. She is trying to bring him to life, literally. She croons, then sings the great Bessie Smith blues song, "Down in the Dumps."*]

Gonna straighten up baby "straighter than Andy Gump." Gonna get it up, babe. Remember your Bible: crucified, but on the third day he *rose*. Let's go, honey, don't cry, baby, don't cry, I know, I know. Let's go home now.

[*They dance.* CIRCE *sings. At first her emphasis is light, then a fierce, growling affirmation.*]

"I'm twenty-five years old
That ain't no old maid
I got plenty of vim and vitality
I know that I can make the grade.

I'm like a tiger
I'm ready to jump
I needs a whole lots of loving
'Cause I'm down in the dumps."

[CIRCE *dances* BRAVO *over to the rocking chair and sits with him on her lap.*]

WALKIE-TALKIE VOICE: "Tower to Field: 2330 hours!..."

CIRCE: Yes, child. Nurse, my Bravo... Gather your strength. Nurse, my wrath...We're an entry now, whatever happens; like Bonnie and Clyde, we're Circe and the Stranger. The "wanted" posters will name us both as "Fugitives from the Camp of Victory" ...Nurse...Listen, Wisconsin, don't die on

me now. This is Circe talking. You're forgiven. You can't help your thoughts any more than I can! Do you copy? Any more than I can...
>   [*Then she rocks and croons her nightmare to* BRAVO.]

And now I'll tell you my nightmare...Ready? Turn on the TV set. Look at it. That's my husband, the President, live on tape. He tells us why it's better to die than to live... "I will be with you; whatever happens, I will not leave this office..." says the Commander-in-Chief — except that he's down below under the mountain sucking up Vichyssoise and trying out the tennis courts with the blue plastic grass... The Commander-in-Chief — he nods to a blue-eyed boy and there in the bowels of the earth the button is pushed at last and in Nevada and Colorado and Wyoming and Nebraska the shark-faced missiles tear up out of their silos... The minutes crawl by. [*with a lump in her throat*] America is over... Can you see it, Bravo? The eyeballs melt, the leaves on the trees explode into flames.
>   [*The sound of the helicopter intrudes.*]

"My fellow Americans. Remember Pearl Harbor!" I see the firestorms and the cosmic clouds. I see a faithful dog and its shadow, flung for ever against a wall of flesh... What do you see, Bravo, underground?

BRAVO: "Eyes only — need to know."
>   [*He crawls away from* CIRCE.]

CIRCE: Wait — I need you to live, to help me before they push that button...
>   [*She crawls after him.*]

BRAVO: ...The earth had four moons in its time. Three crashed to earth destroying all the animals in a volcano of fire and ice.

> [CIRCE *is at his feet. He is like burning ice. His voice rises slowly.*]

The race shrank to nothing. But a few of us hid in the mountains — Aryans and Caucasoids!... Again there are giants among us in the mountains. Theatre Nuclear War is the surgery that will open up the world... This is our credo: We are the Ice Men. We are born to save Western Civilization. Save her from every enemy, including death.

> [CIRCE *huddles next to him.*]

CIRCE: Save us, Bravo —
BRAVO: Too late.
CIRCE: Before they push the button.
BRAVO: No button — Launch on warning.
> [*He flinches.*]
No! — I'm a bomb. Don't push me. Don't touch me. I'm a bomb.
CIRCE: Who pushes the button?
BRAVO: No one.
CIRCE: The button —
> [*The truth is dawning on her.*]
BRAVO: Pushes a button...
> [CIRCE *stares out at the world that is ending.*]
CIRCE: Then there really won't be any Soldiers' Clubs, this time? No flood of sweet 19-year-old semen sweeping the whores of Hattisburg and Alexandria into "houses" of their own, this time? No USO shows, this time? No "Hi, folks, this is Robert-radio-active-Hope," this time?
BRAVO: A million computers killing time! This computer order no.1: kill the dead and the unborn — Program A: occupy Time plus Space. Destroy the past to save it — wipe out the future —
CIRCE: I see it: endless winter.

[*Their voices blend and overlap.*]
To sister...To mother...To father and son and the Holy Ghost.
[*She sings "Bless 'em All" softly.*]

BRAVO: The North Woods are burning. The lakes, the wild rivers, the woods are on fire — The bomb's inside me, there's a bomb inside me!

[BRAVO *pants like an animal. Now the search beam from the hovering helicopter begins to cut across the lodge, in and out, creating a strobe effect. Their voices are rhythmic and pounding.*]

CIRCE: Jesus, Jesus, Jesus...

BRAVO: I'm on fire — The bomb's inside me!

[*The helicopter shakes the lodge. Strobe lights blaze.*]

AARDVARKS and MOWAGS go against KANGEROOS and KITCHENS.* Moscow all gone in 90 seconds, New York in 95.

CIRCE: FAT MAN!*

BRAVO: PAVES and PAWS and SCAPEGOATS. Bring in APHIDS, SPARROWS, WALLEYES —*

CIRCE: LITTLE BOY, FAT MAN — LITTLE BOY, FAT MAN!*

BRAVO: FISHPOTS, THUDS, TWEETS — SCORPIONS, GALOSHES —*

CIRCE:
BRAVO: } FAT MAN!

BRAVO: FISHBED, FLOGGER, FOXBAT, FITTER, FLAGON, FENDER, FIDDLER, FIREBAR, FORGER —*

---

* *Names of nuclear warheads.*

CIRCE: ⎫ HERCULES, STARLIFTER, GALAXY — FAT
BRAVO: ⎭ MAN! COBRAS and SEA KINGS and SEA STALLIONS against HOODLUMS and HORMONES and HINDS — DRAGONS against FAGGOTS — MXs — HALLMARKS!*

> [*The helicopter roars out. Firelight and moonlight.* CIRCE *lies in* BRAVO'*s arms, spent and at his mercy.*]

CIRCE: Is this the Kingdom of the Dead?

> [*The walkie-talkie sputters.*]

WALKIE-TALKIE VOICE: 2350 hours. Able to Bravo, Able to Bravo. Do you copy? It is 2350 hours, do you copy? Do you copy? Do you copy? Do you copy? Bravo, do you copy?...

> [CIRCE *and* BRAVO *remain in a panting tableau as the electronic order continues. But* BRAVO *does not answer. The voice keeps calling* BRAVO *as the moonbeam slowly fades to black on the warm, living, sweat-glistening statue of* CIRCE *&* BRAVO. *In the darkness, after the curtain, the voice keeps demanding "Do you copy?" Then silence.*]

THE END

Also available from Amber Lane Press:

Brian Clark   WHOSE LIFE IS IT ANYWAY?

The play that launched Brian Clark to fame in 1978 when it transferred from the Mermaid to the Savoy Theatre en route for smash-hit success on Broadway. The central character is faced with a future of total dependence on a life-support machine. In his fight to determine the course of his own life – and death – he encounters fierce opposition from the medical profession.

Brian Clark   CAN YOU HEAR ME AT THE BACK?

Brian Clark's second West-End stage play, where he turns his attention to the world of architects and town planners who, instead of designing buildings that fit the human scale, seem only to succeed in creating a succession of 'people filing cabinets'.

Ronald Harwood   THE DRESSER

Michael Billington found *The Dresser* '...a wonderfully affectionate and intelligent play about the theatre. It captures not only the equivocal relationship between star and dresser, it also conveys the bitchiness, the sentiment, the anecdotage, plus the feeling that the backstage world is itself a little kingdom, a tatty Camelot worshipping a prop Holy Grail.' Released as a feature film in 1984, starring Albert Finney and Tom Courtenay.

Ronald Harwood   TRAMWAY ROAD

Set in Cape Town in 1951, one year after the Population Registration Act was passed in South Africa. In the 1950s Tramway Road was a notorious Cape Coloured ghetto located within the predominantly white residential suburb of Sea Point. Ronald Harwood explores the influence that Tramway Road exerts over four characters: an expatriate English couple, Arthur and Dora Langley; Emil, a young man with dreams of becoming an actor in London; and Jacob, a house servant.

Julian Mitchell   ANOTHER COUNTRY

One of the West End's resounding successes of 1982, winning the SWET award for 'Play of the Year'. The setting is an English public school in the 1930's. The two central characters, Guy Bennett and Tommy Judd, are both, in their own different ways, rebels and outsiders who dare to fight against the system.

Julian Mitchell   FRANCIS

Francis of Assisi was a man totally dedicated to a missionary life of poverty and simplicity. He wished to follow the gospels literally and to be a true disciple of Christ. In this play Julian Mitchell writes about the forces that turned Brother Francis into Saint Francis.

Brian Thompson   TURNING OVER

A deliciously funny satire on how television documentaries are made. A BBC film crew is on a hill station in India, making a programme for a series entitled 'I could be happy here'. But the presenter, director and technicians are far from happy as they battle with the climate, the food and the souring relationships.

Hugh Whitemore   PACK OF LIES

Based on the real events surrounding an American couple living in Britain, Helen and Peter Kroger, who were found guilty of spying for the Russians in 1961. The action centres around the Jackson family who as friends and neighbours of the Krogers are drawn into a conspiracy of betrayal.

For a complete catalogue of our plays write or telephone:
Amber Lane Press, 9 Middle Way, Oxford OX2 7LH.
Tel. Oxford 50545